Don't Swear in Church
(unless you really mean it!)

why church membership vows *actually* matter!

JEAN F. LARROUX, III

WESTBOW·
PRESS
A DIVISION OF THOMAS NELSON
& ZONDERVAN

WestBow Press books may be ordered through booksellers or by contacting:

WestBow Press
A Division of Thomas Nelson & Zondervan
1663 Liberty Drive
Bloomington, IN 47403
www.westbowpress.com
1 (866) 928-1240

ISBN: 978-1-4908-3877-9 (sc)
ISBN: 978-1-4908-3876-2 (e)

Library of Congress Control Number: 2014909587

Printed in the United States of America.

WestBow Press rev. date: 6/17/2014

Contents

Acknowledgments

Special thanks to the Robinson family for giving me a place to write and unwind—Hotty Toddy!

Deep appreciation to all the friends who suffered through the early edits, my colloquial style, love of air quotes, words in italics, and shifts from first to third person—"JBarn," Katie and Abbie.

I am particularly indebted to three men whom I have been blessed to watch love Jesus' lambs with great pastoral care and concern: Rev. Bryant Hansen, Rev. Curt Moore, and Rev. Will Spink. Thank you all for teaching me how important these vows are to us and to the bride.

Thanks so much to my wife and other family members who endured many moments of "Not now; I'm writing!" You make me laugh, love coming home, and eagerly await the annual unveiling of the Saints room. *Who Dat!*

Finally, to Melissa, Bob, and Ken, transfer!

Preface: Wedding Vows for Everyone

Imagine yourself standing in front of the church.
Imagine the people gathered in the pews behind you.
Imagine the minister asking you to make vows.
Imagine everyone waiting for your response.
Imagine that you finally muster up the strength to say, "I do."

Now imagine that we're *not* talking about your wedding day.

"I do." These two little words make up the shortest sentence most of us will ever speak, but they are also the weightiest words in our vocabulary. We are all familiar with these two words when a bride and groom standing together at the altar use them, but these are the same words spoken by another bride: the bride of Christ! They are used to express our consent to church membership vows when we become members of the church.

This book is designed to take those two little words and unpack their implications for each of us as church members. It is written for two groups of people: those considering joining the church and those who already have. Whether you have taken these vows or you are about to take these vows, this book is for *you*. This is a tool for contemplation as we consider how soberly we approach our vows.

The church was purchased with the blood of Christ. That great cost compels us to be very clear about what we are saying when we, the bride of Christ, tell Him, "I do."

"No man can have God for his father
and not have the church as his mother."
SAINT AUGUSTINE

Questions, Vows, and Membership—What For?

Let's ask an obvious question: why do we have membership vows at all? Why do we have any membership criteria? Why don't we just all come together in one building and whoever shows up shows up, and there are no members, no membership? Why can't it be like that? It sounds much less exclusive than having to join something or take vows, right?

a very hard

The reason we have church membership is actually quite simple. Christians are referred to as believers. The basis of Christianity is a belief system. Church membership is an acknowledgment by a particular church that the people who are joining the church have a belief system that is consistent with their own belief system. When someone joins the church, he doesn't *become* a believer; he is acknowledged *as* a believer. If someone's beliefs are found to be consistent with the beliefs of a particular church, then such a person is welcomed as a member of that church.

Imagine a hypothetical scenario. Let's say you are the only Christian in a particular city and you have lived as the only Christian there for some time. Imagine that one day, while shopping at the local grocery store, you strike up a conversation with someone. As you make small talk, imagine she says to you something like this: "Well, I'm buying all this stuff because I'm new to town and just getting settled. I have most everything I need, except a Bible. Mine is still packed."

Bells and whistles go off in your head. A Bible? Still packed? Maybe this person owns a Bible for a reason! Remember in our ridiculously hypothetical scenario that you are the only Christian you know. You then ask her, "Why do you own a Bible?" and she responds, "Well, this may sound strange to you since I don't think there are many religious people around here, but I am what they call a 'Christian.'"

More bells and whistles go off. You whisper to her, "Me too!" and she gets a really excited look on her face! As the two of you keep talking, you both pull your carts over to the side and go a bit deeper in the conversation.

"You said you were a Christian, right?"

And she says, "Right!"

"That is unbelievable!" You add, "I have never met someone who believes what I believe."

You probe a little further. "Let me ask you another question. Do you believe that the Bible is God's Word?"

"Yes, I do!" she exclaims.

You reply, "Me too!"

She might ask you in return, "Do you believe that Jesus rose from the dead?"

You say, "Yes, I have believed that since I became a Christian!"

She says, "Me too!"

Then you ask another question, "Do you think that when we Christians die we go to heaven?"

"Yes, I definitely believe that!"

You reply, "Me too!"

That conversation might go on for a while, and after swapping several more "Me too!" comments, the two of you determine that you have the same fundamental beliefs. At that point, you might decide to meet together to worship the same God you both believe in! You decide that Sunday mornings are a good time to meet and make plans for worship *together*.

This little example is much caricatured, but if you take the essence of this scenario and repeat it over and over again, then you have a very crude example of how belief systems are established and how churches begin. Doctrine is not a hurdle erected by man to keep people *out of* the church; it is a clear admission of what a group of people believe who happen to be *inside* a particular church!

Think for a moment how unhelpful it would be for a church to be unclear about its exact beliefs. Imagine attending a particular church for a while and then learning that in all the music for the next month the name *Jesus* was going to be replaced with *Buddha* because many of the other people felt that Jesus and Buddha were both peaceful prophets and deserved equal airtime in the music. You might respond, "Oh, I don't think I believe that. I'm not sure I can affiliate as part of this group anymore since our beliefs are so different."

This principle holds true in a myriad of arenas in life. We affiliate with political parties based on shared beliefs, join service organizations based on shared beliefs, and join fraternal organizations based on shared beliefs. Human beings affiliate on the basis of shared beliefs in countless ways. Affiliating with a church based on shared beliefs is consistent with normal human expressions of affinity.

Suppose someone showed up at a meeting where vegetarians share organic recipes with each other. Imagine the horror in the room if a new person stood up and asked if anyone had a good fried chicken recipe or a great steak marinade. You would quickly learn that you were at the *wrong* meeting. The same would be true if a vegetarian showed up at the local Cattleman's Association wearing a "Meat is murder" T-shirt. In either case, you would have misperceived the purpose of the group and its belief system. Affiliation with that group would be irrational since your personal views were inconsistent with the group's corporate views.

The reason for church membership criteria is exactly the same. We ask questions and respond with answers to ensure that our beliefs and doctrine are the same as the group we are joining. The publicly stated theological views of a particular church allow anyone who says, "I do," to know that they are part of a larger group of people nodding their heads and saying, "Me too!"

Just Jesus and Me

Some people may be able to say "Me too!" to particular theological propositions. Those same folks may even find themselves aligned doctrinally with many other people who believe the same things, but they still might consider formal church membership to be unnecessary. Someone might skeptically think, *Yes, I do believe in Jesus, and yes, I do agree with that doctrine, but being a member of a church isn't necessary to go to heaven so why do I need to join a church? Can't I have a relationship with God with just Jesus and me? I don't have to sit in a building on Sundays to be a child of God! Sitting in McDonald's doesn't make you a Big Mac, and sitting in church doesn't make you a Christian. I don't see what the big deal is about church membership! I think religion is man-made, and I just want to worship God like I'm supposed to—just Jesus and me!* Many people would say amen to the above sentiments.

The skeptic above is right. There is nothing you must say or do in order to be a Christian, other than to believe in Jesus Christ.[1] This question was asked of Jesus in the gospel of John: "What must we do to be doing the works of God?" And Jesus Himself answered, "This is the work of God, that you believe in him whom he has sent."[2] We believe that faith *alone* in Christ *alone* through grace *alone* is what makes a person a child of God. Period. End of story. No disclaimers. *You do not have to be a member of a church to be saved or be loved by God or to go to heaven.* You can be technically converted, call yourself a Christian, and not be a member of a local church—but please keep reading!

Any Christian who would take that last paragraph and use it as personal justification for never joining a church is missing the whole point of his inclusion in the kingdom! It is neither healthy nor good to live disconnected from the body of Christ, the church. You and Jesus together do not make up the perfect church. Half of your church is perfect, and the other half is *you.*

There may be times and seasons when individual believers are not connected to a local fellowship, but unless you are reading this while shipwrecked on a desert island, it is not likely that you are the only Christian for hundreds

---

[1]   It should be said that even the words "believe in Jesus Christ" must have substance to them! What do we mean by "believe"? Is that assent or is it trust? If it is trust, then trust for what? Even the most basic statements of assent and belief *must have theological substance* or they are meaningless.

[2]   John 6:28–29. The Holy Bible: English Standard Version. Wheaton, Ill.: Standard Bible Society, 2001.

of miles. If you can't find someone else who says, "Me too!" with your belief system, then you might need to reexamine your belief system. My pastoral advice to anyone who is disconnected from a local church is that any season of time like that should be short-lived and marked by active pursuit of a local church with which to affiliate!

We need to be members of a local church because we need each other. We need community. We need membership vows because we need to be able to understand and articulate exactly what we mean when we look at a gathered group of fellow believers and say, "Me too!"

Introduction: I Used to Couldn't Spell Presbyterian but Now I Are One …

When someone joins the church, specific questions are asked of him or her. Just before the questions are asked, a charge, similar to the one given to a bride and groom in a wedding ceremony, is often given. The membership charge carries the same weight. Words like *declarations, promises,* and *solemn covenant with God* speak to the significance of the church membership vows. It is a sobering moment where a casual "Me too!" becomes a very solemn "I do" before God.

There are lots of different church flavors. Those flavors come in lots of different denominations: Baptists, Reformed Baptists, Primitive Baptists, Bab-dists, Methodists, Wesleyan Methodists, Episcopalians, non-denominationalists (who are really just Baptists who are allowed to dance), Presbyterians, Reformed Presbyterians, Orthodox Presbyterians, and a thousand others not mentioned.

The specific questions used in the remainder of this book are presently used by the Presbyterian Church in America (PCA) as the basis of membership affiliation and taken from the PCA's *Book of Church Order* (BCO). Other denominations use similar questions with slightly different wording. Although these questions are Presbyterian in origin, they are still helpful for anyone in any denomination that is considering what it means to be a member of a local church. The introduction and questions read as follows:[3]

> All of you being present to make a public profession of faith are to assent to the following declarations and promises, by which you enter a solemn covenant with God and His church.

---

[3] All questions taken from *The Book of Church Order of the Presbyterian Church in America,* 6th Edition. The Office of the Stated Clerk of the General Assembly of the Presbyterian Church in America. Lawrenceville, Georgia. 2009. 57-5.

1. Do you acknowledge yourselves to be sinners in the sight of God, justly deserving His displeasure, and without hope save in His sovereign mercy?

2. Do you believe in the Lord Jesus Christ as the Son of God and Savior of sinners, and do you receive and rest upon Him alone for salvation as He is offered in the gospel?

3. Do you now resolve and promise, in humble reliance upon the grace of the Holy Spirit, that you will endeavor to live as becomes the followers of Christ?

4. Do you promise to support the church in its worship and work to the best of your ability?

5. Do you submit yourselves to the government and discipline of the church and promise to study its purity and peace?

Question 1: How Bad Is It?

Do you acknowledge yourself to be sinners in the sight of God, justly deserving His displeasure, and without hope save in His sovereign mercy?

What is the question asking?

This first question is anthropological. It is asking you a basic question about yourself. Are you willing to admit how bad you really are? Do you really believe that you are a sinner, that you deserve God's wrath, and have no eternal hope unless He has mercy on you?

What isn't this question asking?

It isn't asking anything about how you get saved or what you believe about Jesus. It isn't asking what you believe about the sins of your neighbor or the sins of your ex-wife. It is asking what you believe about *you*. The question behind the question is this: do you contribute anything to the salvation equation? Before you give the Sunday school answer and shout out, "No! Nothing!" go back and read the question. Do you contribute *anything* to the salvation equation? The answer is yes. You do contribute something to the salvation equation. It is spelled s-i-n.

Genesis 6:5 (NIV) says, "Every imagination of the thoughts of man's heart were only evil all the time." Psalm 51 tells us that we are sinful from the moment of conception. Ephesians 2:1 shows our sinful condition by saying we are "dead in our sins and trespasses." Romans 3 echoes these sentiments, stating that there is "no one righteous, not even one." That includes all of us. This is vitally important to understand because right at the outset, this first question removes any hope of our saving ourselves. This question isn't asking anything about salvation. It is asking if you have correctly identified your own need of salvation and whether or not you have identified the primary problem in your life *as yourself.*

Why is this question important?

If you get this question wrong, you get everything else wrong. This is not an overstatement. All of the other membership questions build on your answer to this one question: are you a sinner? Salvation is predicated on a need for deliverance, and we need deliverance because of our sinful condition. According to the Bible, I am the problem, and if I am the problem, I cannot be part of the answer. Church membership is like joining the Mafia. You have to be bad to get in. As sinners, we need protection from ourselves, and these vows bind us together with like-minded people who believe our only hope is God's grace, not our goodness.

A bit deeper …

For those of you who want a little more meat to chew on, consider several implications of this question. The first phrase "in the sight of God" carries significant weight. It is asking if we agree with God's assessment of our condition. This means that we believe God already sees what is in our hearts. We are not saying that we just hit a few moral foul balls back in college; we are declaring that when God looks at our natural hearts, He does not see purity and goodness but rather sin and unrighteousness.

The second phrase, "justly deserving his displeasure," reflects God's response to what He sees. This is a declaration regarding God's justice. He cannot see the sin in our hearts and then un-see it. We are agreeing that when He sees sin, His divine justice demands divine wrath. The word *displeasure* is accurate but should be understood to carry all the weight of God's wrath and anger. The Bible does not describe us as people who are engaged in a mild dispute with our Creator but as people who are at enmity with God. Man is at war with God in his heart, and for that reason, cosmic treason against a holy God must be punished.

Finally, the phrase "without hope save in His sovereign mercy" means that the heavenly judge has examined all the evidence, and we are guilty as charged and have no hope except that He might have mercy upon us.

So what I'm really saying is ...

Do you	This is a statement made by You personally. These are not the words of your parents, spouse, or pastor. Do *you* take ownership of the fact that this is your own self-incriminating testimony?

....

acknowledge yourselves to be sinners	You are placing your hand on the Bible and declaring that you are a sinner, a *really big* sinner! You are not misunderstood, maligned, and misjudged by people who say you have done wrong. You *have* done wrong, a lot of it! You have lied, stolen, cheated, and hated; worshipped, deceived, and lived for yourself; used, manipulated, and wronged others. You have looked straight at God's holy law and dismissed it. You have done this willfully, knowingly, perpetually, cunningly, and spitefully—*and* you are saying the previous statements are just barely scratching the surface of what is *really wrong* in your own heart.

....

in the sight of God,	God knows the truth about you. He sees all the mess. He knows your sins better than you know them. He sees it all. As much as you are able to finesse and deceive everyone else, you know that He really knows. You are good at hiding your sins, especially the secret ones from others. But He sees everything, including the twisted motives and desires behind all the wrong behavior. God even sees you when you hide from Him in your shame.

justly deserving His displeasure	You are personally saying that God would be totally justified to crush you right now. Imagine speaking these words: "I deserve hell. I know the difference between right and wrong, and I regularly choose wrong. If God punished me eternally, there are many things I might say, but the one thing I could never say is I don't deserve it. I have shifted the blame for many of my sins and have gotten away with it. With God, all the blame rightly shifts to me—not to my coworkers, my upbringing, my circumstances, my finances, my spouse, my children, my parents or anything or anyone else. I am responsible, accountable, and culpable for everything I have ever done. I hate to admit it, but this is the truth."
and without hope save in His sovereign mercy	You are saying, "I have implemented many plans to cope with my failures, but none of them are long-term solutions. I have hoped that other people would forget what I have done. I have hoped that God would grade on a curve. I have hoped to be better than my siblings, colleagues, neighbors, and friends, but such hope is really hopeless. My only true hope is that God keeps His word and is a God of mercy, grace, pardon, and forgiveness. His mercy is my only hope."

The question in plain language ...

Who is the biggest sinner you know? If it isn't you, why isn't it? What do you deserve more: God's love or God's wrath? Without God's mercy what hope would you have?

Question 2: Who Can Make It Better?

Do you believe in the Lord Jesus Christ as the Son of God and Savior of sinners, and do you receive and rest upon Him alone for salvation as He is offered in the gospel?

What is the question asking?

This second question is asking if we know about God's solution to our sin problem. It is about salvation. It is asking how someone who has just verbally signed his own death sentence might actually be pardoned. To put this in evangelical terms, it is asking for a profession of faith (i.e., what could be done to save a condemned man who has done nothing during his own trial except nod his head in agreement with the judge?). Do you know and understand that Jesus Christ is God's merciful, sovereign, loving response to your need for salvation?

What isn't this question asking?

It isn't asking a past-tense question about your understanding of salvation, such as "Have you ever asked Jesus into your heart?" It also isn't asking a historical question, such as "Do you remember when you accepted Jesus as your personal Savior?" None of those answers are germane to this question. This question is asking for a *present-tense* answer. "Do you believe?" is asking you for a statement of active trust, not a statement about your spiritual résumé. You may have wonderful memories of walking the aisle as a child at Crooked Oak Baptist Church in Moosejaw, Arkansas, but this is a question about your right-here, right-now trust in Jesus.

Why is this question important?

Man is separated from God by sin; we know that from question 1. God requires two things for mankind to be reconciled to Him. First, the penalty for sin must be paid. Because human flesh sinned against God, punishment for sin had to be inflicted upon human flesh. Therefore, Jesus

5

Christ came in human flesh to take the punishment for His people and died on the cross to pay their debt.

Second, the Law had to be kept perfectly by human beings. This was the requirement God established in the garden of Eden—perfect obedience by human flesh. If Adam and Eve perfectly obeyed God, they and their offspring were promised life. Conversely, their disobedience meant death for us all. Although we disobeyed and sin entered the world, His holy standard never changed. The Law still had to be kept by human flesh. We needed a perfect human law-keeper. Jesus Christ was the only perfect human being who could keep God's Law. This question is asking if we know Him as both penalty-taker for our sins and law-keeper for our righteousness.

A bit deeper …

Most Christians falsely believe that the biggest problem facing human beings is that they haven't accepted Jesus as their personal Savior. But is that really our *biggest* problem? Why did mankind *need* a Savior? Men and women needed a Savior because at the fall they were separated from God the Father. Humanity's problem is not simply that we haven't "accepted Jesus as our personal Savior" but that our heavenly Father has not personally accepted us because we are separated from Him by our sin. Jesus is the *answer* to our separation problem. He makes us acceptable to the Father by giving us credentials that only rightly belong to Him—His righteousness, His goodness, and His access. Restoration to the Father from whom we've been alienated is the essence of what salvation, redemption, and reconciliation are all about.

In membership question 1, we confessed our sin and acknowledged God's just displeasure with us as sinners. Such a declaration should leave us wondering, *If I just confessed my sin and concurrently admitted that God is justly displeased with sinners, then how can I be reconciled to that same God?* The answer is atonement and imputation! Question 2 asks us if we know Jesus, the only one who can provide atonement as the penalty-taker and imputation of righteousness as the law-keeper. The vow asks, "Do you believe in the Lord Jesus Christ as the Son of God, and Savior of sinners …?" When we answer yes to this question, we are declaring that Jesus Christ alone is sufficient to save us from ourselves and restore us to the Father we lost.

So what I'm really saying is …

Do you believe in the Lord Jesus Christ as the Son of God

When you answer this question in the affirmative, you are in essence saying, "I believe that just over two thousand years ago, a virgin named Mary had a baby and that baby was conceived without sin and placed within her womb by the Holy Spirit. I believe that the second person of the Trinity took on human flesh and lived on this earth. I believe that he was fully God and fully man. I believe I will never fully understand that, but I understand from Scripture that it was necessary. I believe that human flesh had to perfectly keep the law and the only way God's perfect law could be kept by human flesh would be if God Himself became man and did it for us. I believe He did that. I believe that human flesh had to be punished for human transgressions. I believe that when Jesus took on flesh and crucified on the cross that this punishment was the punishment that my human flesh deserved. Right here and right now, I actively trust and believe that Jesus Christ is indeed the Son of God. I have faith that His perfect life and atoning death were both substitutes for my imperfect life and my impending death.

*and Savior
of sinners,*

You are declaring to the Word, "I needed atonement and imputation. I believe Jesus atoned for my sins when He willingly sacrificed Himself on the cross for me. Human blood had to be shed for human transgressions, and His human blood was shed for my transgressions and applied to my account. He was the perfect priest and the perfect sacrifice. There is no need for any further sacrifice to be made. I can't add to or take away from His finished work. When He cried out, "It is finished," it was finished *for me.* Christ paid my debt to God in full, and I have been atoned for. I also believe that His imputation saved me. His perfection was imputed to me. Jesus' holiness, perfection, and right standing with God are now mine. Imputation means that God credited me with something that was not mine. That something was the righteousness of Jesus. I have the full rights of Jesus because they have been given to me by faith. I believe that there is no other way to be reconciled to God—not good works, not sincere motives, not other religions, not claiming ignorance. I believe that all of this is a gift that I couldn't earn or merit. It is mine because He is gracious. His grace alone is the reason I am His. Because I believe that this is true, I cannot hold onto my sin and hold onto Jesus at the same time. If I call him "Savior," then that means I need rescuing, saving, and delivering *from* my sin. In calling Him my Savior, I agree that the things He says are killing me are indeed killing me, and I turn from those sins toward Jesus, the only Savior of sinners.

and do you receive and rest upon Him alone for salvation

You are testifying that Jesus is who the Bible says He was regardless of whether you believe it or not, but you are saying that you *do* in fact believe it! God opened your eyes, and you now see Jesus for who He is—Alpha, Omega, beginning, end, lion, lamb, prophet, priest, and king. Receiving and resting upon Him alone is like putting your hand on a Bible and saying, "I believe He is coming again! I believe that I will be in heaven for one reason: Jesus purchased my soul. He died the death my sins deserved and atoned for my sin. He lived the life the law required and imputed that perfect life to my account. I do not believe that I can clean up my act enough to solve my sin problem, and I cannot muster up enough obedience to solve my holiness problem. My soul finds rest nowhere other than in Jesus, not even in my own valiant efforts to save myself."

as He is offered in the gospel?

God's Word matters. It is where you met Jesus and where you keep meeting Him. Everything you know about how to be saved, who Jesus is, who the Father is, and how the Holy Spirit applied all of this to your life you learned from the gospel. You couldn't know Him apart from His word. You met Jesus walking through the pages of His living and active word and it was used by His Spirit in conjunction with a hundred other people, places, and things to open your eyes and introduce you to Jesus Himself.

In plain language ...

Is your faith real? Is your repentance real? Do you live your life turning *from* your sin and turning *toward* your Savior? Does the Bible give you any reason to believe that God loves you other than Jesus Christ's perfect life and atoning death?

Question 3: So Now What?

Do you now resolve and promise, in humble reliance upon the grace of the Holy Spirit, that you will endeavor to live as becomes the followers of Christ?

What is the question asking?

The third question is very practical. You are being asked whether or not anything you have just said will make a difference in your day-to-day life. This is where the rubber meets the road. Will the previous two statements have trajectory in your life, or are they verbal affirmations of something that really won't have a noticeable impact? The reality behind question 3 is this: would anyone ever be able to tell that you said, "I do," to questions 1 and 2?

What isn't this question asking?

This question is not asking if you are promising to be perfect. You just promised twice that you weren't. You also affirmed that there was only one person ever who was perfect, and His name was Jesus. It is not asking if you are promising to *try* to be perfect. It is asking something much more fundamental: What do you plan to do when you aren't perfect? Where will you turn? To whom will you go? Those answers are fundamental to Christianity. Turning to Jesus for deliverance is not a one-time event; it is a regular reality. Trusting in Christ one time isn't called Christianity. It is called hell insurance. Turning to Jesus daily, weekly, and hourly is Christianity. The apostle Paul tells us that such reliance upon Christ and the regular appropriation of His finished work to your own life produces an "aroma" of Christ to the world.[4]

---

[4]   Second Corinthians 2:14–15 states, "But thanks be to God, who in Christ always leads us in triumphal procession, and through us spreads the fragrance of the knowledge of him everywhere. For we are the aroma of Christ to God among those who are being saved and among those who are perishing." The Holy Bible: English Standard Version. Wheaton, Ill.: Standard Bible Society, 2001.

God promises to place His Spirit in the hearts of His children so that when we regularly turn to Christ, we begin to see by-products of His Spirit produced in our lives. This question is not asking if God will love us more if we produce fruit or if His ongoing love is contingent on our perseverance. As Christians, we will begin to see new affections, new desires, and new distastes. We now love what He loves and hate what He hates. We do this because we are loved and accepted as His own, not in order to be loved and accepted as His own. His love and His Spirit placed upon us produce the fruit (substantial, visible evidence of our faith) that comes from His Spirit. Galatians 5 tells us that this kind of fruit is produced in the life of a believer. In question 3, we promise to live a life dependent on His Holy Spirit to produce that fruit!

Why is this question important?

When people make a profession of faith with their lips, it should also show up in their lives. If someone says they have turned from sin *toward* Jesus, then they cannot concurrently and consistently turn toward their sin *instead of* Jesus. If that is the overall pattern of their lives then they are either lying in what they are saying with their profession of faith or lying in how they are living in their propensity to embrace sin. Those are the only two options. When someone professes faith and says, "Me too!" that statement should have an impact in their day-to-day life.

If you stand before the church on a given Sunday and say, "I know you all love Jesus and I know you all hate your sin—me too!" then such a public profession should change how you approach an ethical dilemma on Monday morning. It is the responsibility of professing Christians to strive with all of their hearts to see that the same profession made on Sunday with their lips is made with their lives on Monday with their personal choices!

But what about the Mondays, Tuesdays, or any other days when sinners don't choose holiness, goodness, and truth? What about those days when we choose sin and find ourselves deeply entangled in things that are actually spiritually deadly and not life giving? Take out your highlighter and start highlighting right here: The question for us as Christians is not whether at some point in the future we will sin. We will! The question is this: *Where* will we turn when we do?

Appropriating the cross of Christ and applying His finished work to our sin and failure is a continual and daily process. Applying the finished work of Christ to our hearts on a daily basis is how followers of Christ are supposed to live the Christian life, not just how we are supposed to *begin* the Christian life!

It may seem obvious how we are to appropriate the work of Christ in our lives when we sin and fail, but it is equally important to know how to apply the work of Christ in our lives when we do good things and obey. Appropriating the law keeping of Christ in our lives is a continual process as well. It is a regular habit that must be cultivated in our hearts and learned because we are people who are addicted to offering our own obedience to God. We want to have some type of good work or personal merit to recommend us to the Father. We'd rather have garments woven together by our rigorous obedience than come to God dressed in the righteous robes of Jesus alone! We must have a firm grip on the gospel in order to embrace the words of Isaiah when he said, "All our righteous deeds are like filthy rags!"[5]

The promise to live "as becomes a follower of Christ" doesn't mean living like someone who doesn't need Jesus, but rather living like someone who needs Jesus and is willing to show the world the beauty of Christ against the backdrop of their own failures and against the backdrop of their own successes![6]

---

[5]   Isaiah 64:6. The text in Hebrew literally says that all of our righteous acts are like "filthy menstrual garments." The offensiveness of that imagery is intentional. The Bible makes the point over and over again that we have *nothing to offer God* other than our sin and Jesus.

[6]   I know that someone will misunderstand that statement and think I'm saying that we should go out and freely sin so that we can show people Jesus "against the backdrop of their own failures." You don't have to "go out and sin" to show people Jesus against the backdrop of your failures. You can just simply be honest about the sin that is *already there!* If you cannot think of one sin in your life that needs His grace without thinking you would have to go out and commit another one, then you don't know yourself very well at all.

A bit deeper …

There are five words that should flavor our understanding of this question in every context and discussion: resolve, promise, humble reliance, and endeavor. Every one of these words speaks of inability, not ability. If you have to resolve to do something, then you do not do it naturally. If you have to promise to do something, then you do not naturally perform that duty. If you have to humbly rely on the Holy Spirit, then you are stating at the outset that you have no ability on your own to accomplish the task. Finally, when someone endeavors to do something, that means they are striving toward or leaning into a goal. Endeavoring to do anything implies that you have not arrived at that goal.

Each of these things—resolving, promising, relying, and endeavoring—ultimately produces a changed life. There should be a difference between the lives of a man or woman who professes Christ and the man or woman who does not. One person embraces sin with reckless abandon, has no sense of shame, and never looks back. The other sins but with a deep conviction of heart and a blushing soul. There is not reckless abandon toward sin; there is an aversion against sin by someone who knows that sin is not where life is found. There is also a profound looking back—not just at the poor choices of yesterday but a look back all the way to the cross of Christ and the shameful knowledge that their sins put Him on that cross.

The apostle Paul said, "I have been crucified with Christ. It is no longer I who live, but Christ who lives in me. And the life I now live in the flesh I live *by faith in* the Son of God, who loved me and gave himself for me"[7] (emphasis mine). Unfortunately, too many evangelicals have read that verse and have subconsciously transposed Paul's words to read, "The life I live in the flesh I live by *faithfulness for* the Son of God, who loved me …"

---

[7] Galatians 2:20. The Holy Bible: English Standard Version. Wheaton, Ill.: Standard Bible Society, 2001.

We do not live by *faithfulness for* Jesus.

We live by *faith in* Jesus.

A life of *faith in* Jesus always leads to *faithfulness for* Jesus, but a life of *faithfulness for* Jesus predictably produces a life of *faith in* our own efforts, our own piety, and our own performance. Living by *faith in* Jesus doesn't lead to licentiousness and sinful indulgence; it leads us to the cross of Christ, where licentious desires and sinful indulgences were crucified for us.

Trusting in Christ's work instead of self-effort isn't taking the easy road to avoid dealing with holiness; it is taking a road harder than most are willing to choose. In many ways, it is easier to live by *faithfulness for* Christ than *faith in* Christ. John Calvin thought so. He said, "He who makes the worship of God consist in faith and repentance by no means loosens the reigns of discipline but rather compels men to the course they are most afraid to take."[8]

So what I'm really saying is …

Do you now resolve and promise,

You are making a vow, a resolution, and a promise. You are giving your word that you will strive, exert energy, make great effort, shed blood, and produce blood, sweat and tears toward this end. This is the same thing as someone in court placing their hand on the Bible and solemnly swearing. You are solemnly swearing that this is your personal vow to God made in the presence of his people. You are also giving your word that your 'new membership resolution' is to keep this vow at all costs.

---

[8] Calvin, John. "The Necessity of Reforming the Church." J. K. S. Reid, Editor. Westminster John Knox Press, 2000, 193.

in humble reliance upon the grace of the Holy Spirit,

You are also concurrently stating that all of your best intentions, inclinations, goals, and promises are worthless unless God works in your heart to will and want what He wants. You are stating that you are not a sufficient or trustworthy resource for the task before you. You are confessing that you don't have the strength, stamina, and wherewithal to keep this promise. You will lean into, rest upon, rely upon, and trust in the Holy Spirit, not in your own holy efforts. You are promising to be dependent upon the Spirit, to pray, fast, wrestle, immerse yourself in Scripture, and surround yourself with His people, not because you are holy and pious but because you are weak, failing, and unable to run the race of faith alone! This is a promise to mitigate your own depravity. You are promising that when you start to slip, you will cry out to God as your primary hope, not as a last resort!

that you will endeavor to live

God has given you a new heart. You now want something you never wanted before—to live for Him. You *want to want* holiness. You *want to want* righteousness. You *want to want* personal piety. You are planning and purposing to live for Him, not for yourself. When you find yourself saying, "I just can't do this anymore," then this vow matters. You have preplanned for your own exhaustion, hopelessness, and despair. Endeavoring to live for Him indicates a painful purposing to do something that doesn't come naturally for sinners, but it is now a glorious new affection in your heart. You are promising to purpose a new way of living!

*as becomes
the followers of
Christ?*

Nothing becomes a follower of Christ more than Christ himself. You are promising to call sin sin. You are saying, "I will call my failures my own. I will turn from my sin toward Jesus. My choices will testify that life is not found in the empty cisterns of rebellion but rather in the living waters of Jesus." You are telling the world that you will say, "I'm sorry" and "I was wrong." You will say that to God and others. People making this vow are saying, "I will not defend my poor actions. My hope is in Jesus, not in my ability to shift 51 percent of the blame somewhere else. Because I know what it means to be loved as a poor, needy, and broken sinner, I will love other poor, needy, and broken sinners. I want people to see Jesus in me. Even when others are tempted to make me out to be a good person, I will make sure they know that my life and love for them is plagiarized from Him. It was His idea for me to love them, not mine." This is a promise to refuse the praise of men when they call you humble and a promise to make sure you are encountering the real Jesus enough to be actually humble and not pretentiously self-effacing. This promise says to God, "I want to be different, really different. If I were okay with who I was, then I wouldn't be a Christian. I always have been and continue to be the biggest problem in my own life. I know how to live as becomes a sinner. I long to live as becomes a follower of Jesus."

In plain language ...

Do you promise to live like someone who can't live without grace? Will you lean on the Holy Spirit for daily strength instead of yourself? Will you strive to make sure that when people see your life they see more of Jesus than they see of you?

Question 4: So Why Here?

Do you promise to support the church in its worship and work to the best of your ability?[9]

What is the question asking?

This question is asking, "Why here?" You could make the first three vows at any evangelical, Bible-believing church and be received as a member, but now you are standing at some specific church in some specific city at some specific point in time, so why here? This is where you go from "Me too!" to "We too!" Are you willing to move from a "me" Christianity to a "we" Christianity? Knowing what this specific church believes, knowing all that they hold near and dear and knowing who they are, are you ready to go all in with them as a specific group of people? Are you ready for this specific church to be no longer the church you are visiting but rather the church you are supporting? Will you have *this particular* bride to be *your* particular bride?

What isn't this question asking?

This question is not asking you to promise that you will never visit another church when you are out of town, nor is it asking you to promise that you will never miss a Sunday service in order to attend Bedside Baptist.[10] It is not saying that you will never, ever change churches or move your membership to another church, but it is saying that such a thing will not

---

[9] This may be the first question that gets a little more denominationally or congregationally specific. But regardless of your particular denomination, your specific affection for and support of the local congregation should be an implied or understood part of your membership commitment, *even if* it isn't technically part of the vows in your particular tradition.

[10] This is a joke for all of you who may have attended the "slept-in" service from time to time. I have never actually done so, because I am much holier than other sinners.

happen lightly, flippantly, without very good reasons and very sound counsel from others.[11]

This question also isn't asking you to promise to be at church every time the doors are open or to participate in every ministry that the church supports. The words "to the best of your ability" acknowledge that there are times, seasons, and personal specifics that will likely make one person's level of involvement different from another. However, these same words are affirming that involvement, support, and passion for the church are important. If you believe in what the church is doing and what it is passionate about, then you should have an affinity for it and aspirations to serve with and through it.

Why is this question important?

Church membership is voluntary. There is no coercive force making you join a particular church. So as a noncompulsory, freewill[12] organization, mutual consent is the basis for inclusion. That means you join a church because you believe in what it is about. You are free to self-exclude by not joining, but when you join, you have, by virtue of exercising that choice, declared your support of the mission, vision, and philosophy of ministry of that particular church.

If someone says that they just can't support *this thing or that thing* going on in a particular church, then they must determine whether *this or that* is going to be a deal breaker or whether these are things which can be embraced and accepted.[13] Very candidly, someone should never join a church hoping to transform it into the church they *would like it to be* if

---

[11] Remember question 1, which says we are sinners and are capable of making choices for sinful reasons, even choosing new churches for sinful reasons, right?

[12] The term *freewill* with regard to an organization is not a theological statement but a descriptive one. Obviously, groups of people whose membership is based on criteria that are not freely chosen are not freewill organizations. One cannot choose gender, skin color, or country of origin. Those are some of the non-freewill instances, but joining a particular church or denomination is a choice that each of us is free to make.

[13] Appendix A: Preferences vs. Philosophy has a helpful discussion regarding this topic.

specific changes were made. This would be as unwise as someone walking down the aisle hoping to marry some fictitious new and improved version of their spouse that they hope to see emerge after the wedding! In a wedding ceremony, words like "richer or poorer," "sickness and health," "good times and bad" are used intentionally to indicate that the commitment of marriage is not a momentary and light decision. Church membership should be approached the same way. If you cannot love the bride as she is, then you should not walk the aisle.

An old marriage proverb says, "Choose thy love and love thy choice." That statement applies to marriage vows *and* membership vows. Imagine that phrase being used in wedding ceremonies *and* in church membership classes. Question 4 is asking if you are willing to choose this church, then are you willing to love thy choice?

A bit deeper ...

Go back to our earlier illustration of the two Christians meeting on the street, where one describes his beliefs and the other says, "Me too!" Is there any reason for either person to say "Me too!" unless a substantive, ongoing relationship with shared purpose, passion, and principles is intended?

Of course, people can have casual agreements about football or holidays where saying, "Me too!" might simply be a cordial acknowledgment of shared interests. Two people wearing New Orleans Saints jerseys might see each other on the street and scream, "Who Dat?" Or two people wearing Christmas sweaters might say, "Merry Christmas," but when two people connect on a spiritual and theological level, there is something more than a holy high five going on, right? Candidly, if there is no intention on the part of someone joining a particular church to *support that church in its worship and work,* then there is no reason to join that church.

The key word in that last sentence is *join.* Welcoming guests and visitors to worship services, fellowship events, and programs with no pressure to join should be part of a congregation's ethos. People should be able to consider their personal motivations for membership without feeling coerced into commitments they don't truly embrace. Accelerated or premature attempts at harvesting members from a list of attendees can lead to members whose commitment is no greater than their desire to remove the stigma of "visitor."

Church *growth* does not equal church *health*. Moving people from attendance rolls to membership rolls does not cultivate church vitality. Church vitality is cultivated when *existing members* and those *considering membership* soberly evaluate and embrace the substance of their vows! Numbers do not matter. There is a bigger goal in the kingdom of God than bigger churches. It is the restoration of all of creation—mankind restored to God and each other! That takes more than sermon spectators. It takes committed Christians who are willing to give their lives *to* Jesus and *for* each other. When people like that join together on the basis of *mutual* vows, the gates of hell begin to loosen on the hinges!

This vow to *support the church in its worship and work* also includes financial support. I made a decision a few years ago to start inviting visitors to *not participate* in the financial offering during worship. I actually told them from the pulpit that we *did not expect* them to give any money. I told them to keep their wallets and checkbooks closed. I made sure they knew that we loved having them visit with us, but that it was not their responsibility to fund the work of the church. I did not want anyone to think that we were hoping they'd leave a big check before they left the building.

Concurrently, I reminded *our members* of the privilege they had to support the church in its worship and work. God used both of those exhortations to do two things: He stirred the hearts of our members to respond to His blessings by giving tithes and offerings and He stirred the hearts of many visitors to *become* members and begin giving. From the standpoint of loving our neighbors, many of the new members mentioned later that one of the first things they could not shake out of their minds about our church was the encouragement to *not* give. They became convinced that they were loved by the church as people created in the image of God, not simply as potential donors. From the standpoint of church membership, people were convicted that their vows and their giving mattered. There is nothing profound about any of this. The reasoning is very simple: if it is *your* church, then it must be *your* church, period. No visitor or guest has ever promised anything to the church, but all of the members *have*. We have sworn before God that in good times, bad times, sickness, health, poverty, and wealth, we will love and care for *His* bride. We shouldn't swear in church unless we really mean it!

So what I'm really saying is …

Do you promise to support the church

You are making a promise along with everyone else who has said, "Me too!" that you are committed to *this particular church*. Support means personal, financial, verbal, and physical support. Some may have more to give than others. This will depend on the stage and season of life, but all can give something. Support doesn't simply mean volunteering or giving or teaching; it means that each person, according to how God has blessed and equipped them, is intentional about using their gifts to benefit His bride.

Aside: This membership question is closely tied to the next membership question, but suffice to say at this point that we usually express our pleasure or displeasure with decisions in the church by giving or withholding support. It is vitally important that we recognize vow 4 to be independent of our opinions about leadership decisions. This is our solemn promise to support the church not just when the decisions of the church are ones that we like.

in its *worship and* *work*	Churches gather together corporately to worship God. We vow to participate in that corporate gathering. We are promising to engage, sing, and open our hearts to the Word of God preached, sung, and prayed. This means showing up, helping your family show up, and making worship a priority in your lives. This isn't legalism; this is passion. The church also has ministries and mission work that extend beyond Sunday morning worship. This is the "work" of the church. You are promising to find a place in the church where you are gifted to serve and then jump in with both feet. You could also ask church leaders to help you find somewhere outside the four walls of your church that needs your passion, service and talent. You can serve Jesus in lots of places in the kingdom as an extension of the bride you have chosen.
to the best of *your ability?*	Subjectively, only you can determine what the 'best of your ability' means. Only you know what you can do at any given time. God alone is Lord of your conscience. This frees us from living under the disappointed glances and verdicts of others who think you aren't doing enough. It frees you from having to explain yourself when you are late for worship or feel obligated to tell others why you've missed the last three weeks of church. You don't have to tell everyone some sob story about you helping poor, starving, needy salespeople at the national sales meeting in Hawaii … Seriously, God is the judge of the heart. You are free from the verdicts

of yourself, your own guilty conscience, and the verdicts of other men. Therefore, and this is the kicker, you are *actually really free to determine what you can and cannot do to the best of your ability*. When you don't *have to have* the applause or approval of others because you already have His approval, then you will honestly put in *more* time, effort, and heart than you would have ever put in if you were just checking some obligatory box. You are free to do all of those things with tremendous zeal because you know you already have His approval! Box-checking Christianity produces bare-minimum Christians. Real grace always leads to unfettered, joyful, and sacrificial service! Your promise is to expose your heart to enough of His grace that you can honestly answer this question without moving toward guilt-driven obedience!

In plain language ...

Will this church be a different place because you joined it? Because the church is a place for the guilty to live guilt-free and the selfish to give their lives away, will you worship, work, laugh, cry, serve, repent, and share your life with us if we promise to do the same with you?

Question 5: I'm Saying What?!?

Do you submit yourselves to the government and discipline of the church and promise to study its purity and peace?

What is the question asking?

This question is asking, "Do you trust God to lead you and your church through the leadership He has put in place?" This is the most difficult vow to keep. It includes a word that *feels like* a four-letter word: *submit*. We don't like this word. We don't even like this concept, unless of course we are talking about other people submitting to us. This question is asking if we have enough trust in God's leadership, direction, and oversight of the church to embrace decisions that we did not personally make and may not personally like. The word *submit* really *feels like* a four-letter word even in church.

What isn't this question asking?

This question is not asking you to be mute, to never ask questions, to never ask why, or to walk around the church like robots who simply do whatever the leaders of the church tell you to do. That is called a cult, not a Christian church. This question isn't asking you to promise that you will never, ever disagree with decisions that are made. It isn't asking to you to make a vow that you will always like every song choice, carpet color, or Sunday school class. It isn't asking you to put on a fake Christian smile and pretend to everyone that you are joyful. It is, however, asking you to do one thing. When you disagree with your church leadership, will you ask God to deal with your rebellious heart before you spend time, effort, and energy dealing with the decision you don't like?

Why is this question important?

Submission only matters when you disagree. People don't need to submit to things they agree with; those things are just embraced! Who doesn't

26

love doing things they agree with? Imagine a father making this statement: "Children, it is important that you submit to me in the decision that I have made as your father. I have determined that we will have ice cream every night after dinner. No talking back. I don't want to hear your excuses. You will eat this ice cream, or so help me ..." Ummm. That's ridiculous, right? But what if we replace the words *ice cream* with *brush and floss your teeth*? Now the battle begins, right? That is where submission matters, in the places where an individual might have some distaste or disagreement.

As sinners, it is very important for us to understand the weight of this question because there are two significant areas of life in the church where we are likely to disagree. This question addresses both of those areas.

The first area of potential disagreement is the area of church "government"—how things are determined and decided. We have all seen decisions made in the church or in other organizations that we immediately thought were really bad decisions. We have even given input to leaders in those organizations advising them of the potential pitfalls of our perceived bad decisions. We have suggested that such decisions were, in our opinion, shortsighted or misguided. We've spoken to other opinion leaders and influential parties in those organizations about those decisions, and even then, despite having given everyone the "benefit" of our counsel and wisdom, the *wrong* decisions were still made, right? That is where submission matters. It matters most in the places where we must acknowledge that God's authority in the church is higher than our own and that His authority is exercised through the leadership of the church, not through us individually.

It should be noted that our sinful temptation is often to give the appearance of submission while subtly protesting. This is where we appear to "submit" but still actually make our disagreement known by withholding our financial support to the church or by pulling back from service in a particular area. Such "submission" is not submitting at all. It uses words like *submit*, but it is actually self-deception at best and manipulative coercion at worst. It is even possible to rebel against a decision by constantly telling and retelling everyone how you are committed to submitting *to bad decisions* and asking others to pray for you. Even talking to "just a few people" about our struggles can still spread seeds of dissension by making sure everyone knows how much you are struggling with the decisions being made.

The second area where we are likely to disagree has nothing to do with decisions made for the entire church. It has to do with decisions made for our own personal lives. This is where the other word that *feels like* a four-letter word comes in: *discipline.* In this vow, we promise to submit to the government *and discipline* of the church. This is a complicated subject and could be the subject of an entire book, but suffice to say that submitting to church discipline is basically personal accountability to whether or not we really believe that we are so sinful that we could deceive ourselves into thinking that sin was safe.

A bit deeper …

In question 1, we admitted that we are people whose judgment is suspect and tainted with sin. In this vow, we are asking that a very specific course of action be implemented if we dive headlong into beliefs or behavior that are contrary to God's Word. Our plain-language version of question 1 said,

> Who is the biggest sinner you know? If it isn't you, why isn't it? What do you deserve more: God's love or God's wrath? Without God's mercy what hope would you have?

We confess that we are wicked from the moment of conception, born dead in our sins, and deserving of God's wrath in our natural state. Jeremiah 17:9 says, "The heart is deceitful above all things and desperately wicked. Who can know it?" Jeremiah is saying that we are *so sinful* that we are even capable of self-deception. Rev. Hal Farnsworth of Redeemer Presbyterian Church in Athens, Georgia, is known for asking, "If you were deceived, would you know it?" His question is simple and rhetorical, but his point is profound. The very nature of self-deception presupposes that the first person to be blinded and deceived by sin is the sinner himself! If part of our sinful nature means that we are capable of self-deception, then one of the things we need from the leadership in the church is their willingness to help us see our sin when we don't or won't see it! This matters the most when we have deceived ourselves into thinking that our sinful behavior is safe to embrace!

Church discipline is the process of directing people back to the cross of Christ when they falsely believe that they don't need the cross of Christ. Self-deceptive hearts are prone to believe the lie that life can be found in sin, not in Christ. Remember *submission only matters when we disagree.* This includes disagreements about whether or not we are living in sin and whether or not specific behaviors are sinful! The primary times when we would have to be called to submit to the discipline of the church regarding our sin are *precisely those times when we don't think we are in sin!* This vow is like a spiritual insurance policy against self-deception.

Imagine making a public statement like this: "Attention, everyone in my new church family. I thought you should know something about me. I am a self-deceiver. I lie to myself. I think I'm always right, and I especially think I'm right when I'm doing something wrong. If you want to see me get really defensive, then point out my sin when I don't want it pointed out. I will fight you tooth and nail, but please be aware of something. The more that I try to deny my sin and keep it in the darkness, the more *I need you* to help bring it into the light. Fight *for* me, not *with* me. Battle for me even if it feels like it is against me. Please pray for me. If I am kicking, screaming, and throwing punches, then please know I am not thinking clearly. I am telling you this now while I am thinking clearly, because I know that when that time comes, I will be blind to what is going on. I am asking you to step in. Spiritually tackle me to the ground. Help me to detox from my sin. Help me to starve myself from the poison I have been gorging myself on. Be gentle, but please help me see the consequences of my sin. Be loving enough to help me to see what I can't see. This is the vow I'm making to you: if all of you see my sin clearly and I don't see it, then I give you my word today that I will trust your word and not mine. In those moments, *you will be right* and *I will be wrong,* but don't forget I won't see it *then.* So please don't give up on me! Pursue me. Pray for me. Challenge me and love me back to Jesus. Please help me remember that my sins cost Jesus His life, and I cannot find life in the same place that brought about His death. Do not let me profane the name of Christ or pollute what He has done for me."

Imagine the preceding paragraph read aloud and signed by each person joining the church. Imagine that signed statement placed in a glass box with each member's name on it, bearing these words: "In case of self-deception, break glass." That is what it means to submit to the discipline of the church.

So what I'm really saying is ...

Do you submit yourselves to the government

Are you willing to be *under authority* in the church not just *in authority* over the church? You may be "in charge" at work, at home, or in lots of other places, but can you leave your throne at home when you come to church? There is only one King in the church, and His name is Jesus. This applies to church officers too! None of you, on your own, speak for Jesus. We believe that any church power is held jointly as a group, not by the members individually. Can you submit to that? Submission will only matter when you disagree, so think long and hard about this vow. It is not likely that you will have to remember these vows until your blood pressure is rising about something you don't like. Can you keep your word *then* when it really matters?

PS: submission also applies to attitudes, actions, and things like grumbling, gossiping, eye rolls, exhales, head wags, and I-told-you-so's!

*and
discipline*

How much do you distrust yourself? You said in vow 1 that your heart was capable of self-deception. Do you really believe that? Do you want us to step in if we see you putting yourself in spiritual danger? If we do that, you probably won't like it. You probably won't like us. You will probably try to make excuses or blame someone else. You will probably withdraw from us. You might even try to join a different church and tell them that we didn't love you. Do you want us to keep after you? Do you want us to keep directing and redirecting you to turn back to Jesus? Do you want us to remind you that the issue is your sin and caution you from blaming your behavior on the sins of other people instead? Are you asking us to escalate our discipline if you become combative or belligerent?

We promise to be patient, loving, and gentle, but are you telling us that your spiritual life is so important to you that you want us to use every possible means at our disposal to warn you if you seem unresponsive? That may mean that we have informal meetings and formal processes, and it might even mean that we should forbid you from taking communion because of your rebellion. We know that steps like that seem extreme right now, but if we see that you are living your faith in a way that is wholly inconsistent with your promise to turn from sin and toward Jesus, do you want us to protect the integrity of the Lord's Table and turn you away from it? Please know that we would only do so in order to help you see and feel in a very tangible way the danger you are in! That would be our goal!

31

As an utter last resort, and as a sobering warning to you and the church, if you persist in your sin, persist in rebellion, reject our counsel, reject our calls to repentance, and become indifferent to the Lord's table and harden your heart, are you asking that we make the heartbreaking acknowledgment that you are no longer professing the same faith we profess? You became a communing member of this church *by profession of faith* and we would have to declare that we no longer believe you are professing that faith or trusting in Christ if we had to excommunicate you from our fellowship. Do you understand the weight of that reality? We would only do that if we were fully convinced that although you once said, "Me too!" that now you are clearly and consistently saying, "Not me!" Do you understand that the last thing we would ever want to do is to excommunicate you from this church? But we would do it with tears in our eyes and broken hearts as an utter last resort because we love Jesus and His gospel more than we love anything else.

....

of the
church,

The only power that a church has is moral and spiritual. The church cannot enforce compliance with any counsel given to you or decision made. That means we can't *make you* do anything. We can encourage you. We can exhort you, but ultimately, submission in the church is about God subduing your heart, not us physically restraining your behavior. Do you understand that? Do you believe that the church is God's chosen vehicle to lead you, protect you, and spiritually care for you? Do you acknowledge that this church is the one you are choosing to affiliate with and that you are asking *this body* to be the primary spiritual context where God will guide, direct, discipline, disciple, encourage, and love you as a Christian?

....

and promise to study its purity and peace?

Do you know that these two things go hand in hand? The church's doctrinal and ecclesiastical purity is important to God, our Father. The church's corporate peace and communion with each other are also His passions. Will you study (which means work for, seek after, familiarize yourself with, and strive toward) both the purity and the peace of the church? If heresy arises, will you disturb the peace of the church for the sake of her purity? If the peace is disrupted by sin, will you call her back to the purity of the gospel? Will you study doctrine and delve into the truth of His word in order that you will know the difference between pure and impure doctrine? This means that you won't believe every wind of doctrine that blows around or every "Christian" book that is published. You are promising to evaluate what you read and believe against His Word, not simply to believe something because it showed up with the highest page ranking on a Google search. Will you begin your work for the peace of the church by starting with your own heart, your own motives, and your own propensity to disrupt relationships?

Jean F. Larroux, III

In plain language ...

Can you bow the knee to anyone other than yourself? Can you trust godly leadership instead of spiritual self-government? Can trust that leadership when it comes to church decisions *and* personal choices? Do you love the church enough to speak up for purity and peace, even if you are the only one who has to speak up?

Where the Rubber Hits the Road

As you may have already noticed, there are likely many churches in your community with whom you might fundamentally agree on faith issues. There may be many local congregations with whom you could say, "Me too!" You may actually have true philosophical alignment with several different churches, even several churches of the same denomination in your city. How then are you supposed to discern which particular church is the best for you to affiliate with as a member? That is a good question!

Preferences vs. Philosophy

Let's do another hypothetical exercise. For our purposes now, we are assuming that you already hold to all of the basic beliefs we have outlined. You know your sin. You know Jesus. You love the church as an institution and are willing to submit to whatever leadership is present in whatever church you choose, but as of yet, you have not chosen a *specific* church to join.

The analogy below is intended to illustrate the interplay between preferential issues and philosophical issues that will affect your choice when you are finally choosing a particular church to call home.

Pretend that someone must find a home, apartment, or condominium to live in. While looking for a place to live, that person will likely find a real estate professional to help him. In order to find that home, the real estate agent would ask the potential buyer lots of questions. The agent would want the buyer to identify the things that he "must have" (i.e., nonnegotiables/things he is philosophically committed to having) and those things that would be "nice to have" (i.e., negotiables/preferences).

The Realtor inquires, "You said you want to buy a house, but do you want two stories or one?" Imagine our fictitious buyer says, "Oh, we must have one story, because our son has limited mobility and cannot use stairs." The group of potential houses has just narrowed down and likely ruled out most condos and apartments, at least all the ones with stairs. *A one-story house is identified as nonnegotiable.*

"What about a pool?" the agent asks.
"Oh, we definitely want a pool! That is one of the few exercises that really allows our son to get a full workout with his condition and have great cardio stimulation!" *The number of choices narrows again as another nonnegotiable is identified.*

Then our buyer chimes in with more input. "Oh, and I'm a gourmet cook, so I have to have a cook's kitchen with a gas stovetop. Nonnegotiable!" The potential number of homes narrows again. Apartments are now ruled out, and we have three very specific nonnegotiable things we are looking for in this new home: one story, pool, and a cook's kitchen.

We could continue the exercise, but you get the point. When we are done, we will have a group of dwellings to choose from that fit the stated nonnegotiables of this family. Things like paint color, carpet, and amount of grass to cut would not be deal breakers, so we would consider those items to be negotiables.

When it comes to joining a particular church, you should clearly establish what your nonnegotiables are. Does the church have to be a particular denomination? Does the music have to be a certain style? Does the worship have to be liturgical? Are you dead set on having communion every week? Once you establish these criteria, you have established your philosophical nonnegotiables for a church choice, but let me offer a word of warning here. When we are shopping for new homes, God has not told us how He feels about the number of bathrooms we must have or whether or not we should have a pool. To a large degree, even our nonnegotiables in buying a home are simply *firmly determined preferences.* When considering joining a church, you must always hold your philosophical nonnegotiables up to Scripture and ask if *your* nonnegotiables are the same as *God's* nonnegotiables. Sometimes, we are willing to die on a sword that Scripture has not made an issue of life or death. The Bible doesn't say whether or not the minister should wear a robe to preach in. You might *like* that, but before you make that the determining factor in joining a church, make sure you are self-aware enough to acknowledge that some things on your list may not be "thus saith the Lord" issues but rather "thus saith your own preferences."

From the church's standpoint, the membership vows represent the clearly delineated and publicly expressed nonnegotiables for that particular church. If you can answer those questions in the affirmative, then all other issues can be navigated. Notice that the questions don't ask you if you will sing in the choir, teach Sunday school, promise always to wear a suit to church, or home-school your kids. Those things don't make or break your profession of faith, so they don't make or break your admission to the fellowship of the church! All of those other things are negotiable, but the truths expressed in the vows are at the very core of what church membership means. That is why they are *nonnegotiable*.

Churches should strive for the same self-awareness that individuals have with regard to their chosen "personality." It might be that most of the members of the church are young couples with no kids, but that does not mean that a middle-aged couple without children who shows up to church dressed up should feel like they are obligated become hipster in order to fit in. We must be suspicious of baptizing our preferences into philosophical commitments, whether we are members of a church or looking for a church. By the same token, individuals with preferences or passions unlike those of the majority of members of a particular church should not demand or expect a church whose ethos is hipster to act, feel, or seem more yuppie just because they have joined or begun attending that particular church.

From the church's standpoint, the basic membership questions are only designed to establish a basis of affiliation with regard to the nonnegotiables, not to make an exhaustive list of all of the negotiables. This is very important because often when there is a conflict in the church regarding the negotiables (carpet color, music choices, etc.), the church must be able to appeal back to the nonnegotiables as a basis for unity and charity. While church and denominational schisms do still occur over nonnegotiable issues of orthodoxy, more often than not, church splits and squabbles about negotiables can be just as painful and difficult to endure. Self-awareness on the part of any particular church regarding style, preference, and negotiable matters can aid greatly in forestalling and protecting the church against division. Such self-awareness, when it leads to clear self-disclosure regarding those philosophy of ministry issues, allows people from different walks of life, backgrounds, and preferences to understand at the outset who a church *is* and who it *isn't*.

When the nonnegotiables have been clearly established as a mutually agreed upon basis of affiliation, then matters of preference can be discussed, voted on by the church (depending on your tradition), or determined by the leadership. Regardless of the decision-making process, *the determination of negotiable matters, such as carpet color, curtains in the fellowship hall or guitars in the sanctuary, must always be subordinated to the nonnegotiable issues that were the basis of initial affiliation.* Individuals may disagree about negotiable issues and theoretically live happily under one steeple, but disagreement about nonnegotiables is not a matter of preference; it is a matter of philosophy and orthodoxy. It is fine to think that some piece of furniture in the church foyer is outdated; it is much different to think that the concept of the resurrection is passé.

I offer one last word of advice. If someone changes their nonnegotiables while living in the house, major issues will arise. Suppose you have been living in a home for five years but then decide that a home with a pool is too much hassle and you no longer want a pool. At that juncture, you either have to fill in the pool or consider other housing options. That is a painful realization. In either case, you are changing your nonnegotiables, and by implication, you are changing the home you live in. It is "changed" by either transforming the existing home into what you want (by filling the pool in) or changed by leaving the existing home "as is" and transforming your surroundings to meet your new preference (by moving to the new home you have now decided is *now* a nonnegotiable.)

The theological realm is not as easy to navigate as pools, kitchens, and houses. It is easier to see the clear difference between matters of personal preference and philosophical commitment when we are talking about less-emotional issues, such as swimming pools, rather than talking about strongly held theological beliefs. Spiritual issues are always issues of deep personal passion, and it is incumbent upon churches to be clear and up front about who they are in order for potential members to be sure of what they are buying into. Clear communication of nonnegotiable expectations to potential church members allows everyone to know on the front end what is expected so there are no surprises after you "move in."

Beyond the membership questions, conversations with pastors or church officers about the philosophy of ministry, programs, worship styles, and other elements *beyond theology* that make up the ethos of a particular church are profoundly helpful. Potential churches should be asked if there are subtle things you might be expected to do or believe in order to fit in at that particular church. Churches can have unwritten codes of conduct that have started to feel "normal" to them.[14] They may have plenty of nonnegotiables, but they may simply be unaware of the shared assumptions under which they have been operating. Like our marriage vows, church membership vows create a covenant that affects everyone involved.

---

[14] For example, asking questions about schooling options for children (i.e., home school vs. private school vs. public school) is helpful. Unearthing political expectations (i.e., do people assume that you would vote a certain way as a member of that church?) can be very eye-opening. Asking questions about Christian liberty issues, such as having a glass of wine with dinner, will help you know what is culturally acceptable in that congregation. You would want to know whether or not wearing blue jeans to worship would make you seem disrespectful to other members of the church. You would also want to know if wearing a coat and tie would make people wrongly assume you are acting "holier than thou."

Afterword: You May Now Kiss the Bride

You have been looking back and contemplating your own church membership vows, or you may be planning to stand before a church and be asked questions similar to these before you are admitted as a member.

Remember something: church membership is a privilege, not a right. Church membership is a blessing, not a burden. Church membership is an acknowledgment that you *already are* the bride of Christ, not the establishment of that reality.

The very first vow you take tells the world what a miracle it is that you are even standing in a church at all. The rest of the questions should continually humble and amaze us. We confess that we have a perfect God whose perfect justice is satisfied. We have a Savior who has accomplished everything on our behalf. We testify that all this has been given to us as a gift by His grace. We didn't earn it. When the church acknowledges that your testimony is the same as theirs, then you have the privilege of immediate acceptance into His family! They will all be nodding their heads with you saying, "Me too!"

God is your Father. Jesus is your Bridegroom. The church is His beloved bride, and by profession of faith, you are made part of that church. Rejoice when you kiss the bride and say, "I do."

Appendix A:
The Five Questions in Plain Language

Question 1

Who is the biggest sinner you know? If it isn't you, why isn't it? What do you deserve more: God's love or God's wrath? Without God's mercy what hope would you have?[15]

Question 2

Is your faith real? Is your repentance real? Do you live your life turning *from* your sin and turning *toward* your Savior? Does the Bible give you any reason to believe that God loves you other than Jesus Christ's perfect life and atoning death?[16]

Question 3

Do you promise to live like someone who can't live without grace? Will you lean on the Holy Spirit for daily strength instead of yourself? Will you strive to make sure that when people see your life they see more of Jesus than they see of you?[17]

---

[15] Reference original question taken from *The Book of Church Order of the Presbyterian Church in America,* 6th Edition. The Office of the Stated Clerk of the General Assembly of the Presbyterian Church in America. Lawrenceville, Georgia. 2009. 57-5. Question 1: "Do you acknowledge yourselves to be sinners in the sight of God, justly deserving His displeasure, and without hope save in His sovereign mercy?"

[16] cf. BCO 57–5, question 2: "Do you believe in the Lord Jesus Christ as the Son of God, and Savior of sinners, and do you receive and rest upon Him alone for salvation as He is offered in the gospel?"

[17] cf. BCO 57–5, question 3: "Do you now resolve and promise, in humble reliance upon the grace of the Holy Spirit, that you will endeavor to live as becomes the followers of Christ?"

Question 4

Will this church be a different place because you joined it? Because the church is a place for the guilty to live guilt free and the selfish to give their lives away, will you worship, work, laugh, cry, serve, repent, and share your life with us if we promise to do the same with you?[18]

Question 5

Can you bow the knee to anyone other than yourself? Can you trust godly leadership instead of spiritual self-government? Can trust that leadership when it comes to church decisions *and* personal choices? Do you love the church enough to speak up for purity and peace, even if you are the only one who has to speak up?[19]

---

[18] cf. BCO 57–5, question 4: "Do you promise to support the Church in it worship and work to the best of your ability?"

[19] cf. BCO 57–5, question 5: "Do you submit yourselves to the government and discipline of the Church, and promise to study its purity and peace?"

Appendix B: Discussion Questions

These six sets of discussion questions could be used to supplement an existing church membership curriculum.

Note: Following these discussion questions, a suggested twelve-session study plan for smaller groups is included. Working through the group exercise for each chapter would allow small group leaders to potentially lead their groups through six two-hour sessions or twelve one-hour sessions.

Discussion for Question 1: How Bad Is It?

1. How important is question 1 in this discussion of church membership and vows? Why might we say that all the other questions hinge on the answer to this one question?

2. There is something within each one of us that does not seem to mind a *general* statement about our sinfulness (i.e., "All have sinned and have fallen short of the glory of God."). What is it that we particularly dislike about moving from a general confession to specific confession about things that are true of me as an individual?

3. If people were asked this question as it is written "in plain language," how many people do you think would pause and really think about how they were going to answer this? Why might people think twice about whether to be honest about their answers to this question?

4. First John says that if we "claim to be without sin we deceive ourselves and the truth is not within us." Knowing that there are few churchgoing people who would *technically* claim to be "without sin," what are some of the ways that we might *practically* deny being the 'biggest sinner we know'?

5. We said that the church and the mafia are the only two organizations in the world where you have to be bad to get in. What does that mean?

6. The words "justly deserving His displeasure" are used in vow 1. What is the significance of saying that God is *justly displeased* with us? How does this phrase take our acknowledgment of sin one step further?

7. Most prisons are filled with self-proclaimed "innocent men" who were "unjustly accused." When confronted with your sins, do you respond like an innocent man unjustly accused or a convicted criminal who knows his crimes and can own them?

Discussion for Question 2: Who Can Make It Better?

1. Acknowledging we are sinners who are justly condemned would be spiritual suicide if it were not for Jesus Christ. What does it mean to *actively believe and trust* in Jesus?

2. As sinners condemned before God, we had two specific areas that needed to be addressed: our law breaking (See Romans 3:23.) *and* our law keeping. (See Leviticus 19:2.) How did Jesus address both? (See 2 Corinthians 5:21.)

3. Is Jesus Christ the *only way* that someone can be saved?

4. While we might agree that Jesus, not Buddha, Mohammed, or some other prophet, is sufficient to save, most of us trust another Savior regularly. Who is that? Why is that so deadly? What are some of the ways that we *practically* trust in and rely on our favorite substitute Savior called "self"?

5. We declare in this vow that we "receive and rest" upon Jesus alone. Is this question asking for your historical spiritual résumé or your current status update? What is the *present value* of the blood of Christ in your life?

6. What should it look like for us to "rest" in Jesus? Give some examples. Where is one area that you are currently *not* resting? What is keeping you from collapsing onto Jesus?

7. Pair up with someone in the group. Tell them some struggle or sin that you have been dealing with (Use good judgment here!), and then have them declare to you what the gospel says to sinners like you! Next: reverse roles.

8. Do number 7 again, but *this time* tell your partner some spiritual discipline or goal that you have been trying to accomplish. Have the other person describe to you Jesus' perfect obedience on your behalf. For instance, the other person may have been planning to fast for a season of time but has found it difficult. Remind them of all the places where Jesus perfectly obeyed on their behalf. Next: reverse roles.

Discussion for Question 3: So Now What?

1. Are you ever going to get the Christian life "right"? How can you promise and resolve to do something you know you will never be able to do perfectly?

2. Why should the word *endeavor* be encouraging to us?

3. Choosing to love what God loves and hate what He hates is a significant choice. It is also *very* counterintuitive. How is the Holy Spirit intimately involved in this process?

    Note: Think about how the Holy Spirit moves and works in our lives. It is easy to make Him the "mascot" for our Christian lives instead of the means by which we are empowered.

4. How would you like others to respond if they personally see you endeavoring to live *according to your own passions and desires*? Role-play the specific way you would want to be approached by someone who loved you but was worried about your life choices.

5. What is the difference between resolving to rely on the Holy Spirit and resolving to exert more personal self-effort?

6. Practically, what are some of the ways we can move toward Jesus and away from our sinful desires?

7. When you repent, do you find yourself turning to Christ for forgiveness or turning to the opposite of your sin instead? What is the difference between penance and repentance? Do you go to God with promises to "never again" commit your sins or trust in His promise to "never forsake" you, even though you may have sinned?

8. This vow has practical implications for our lives. Someone may be of the opinion that living with their girlfriend outside of marriage is not a big deal, but a biblical view of purity would dictate otherwise. How does living "as becomes a follower of Christ" equate to living as Christ would prescribe? Do you see inconsistencies in your life in this area? Note: If we are honest, we all see inconsistencies in this area, but the real question for each of us revolves around our response to the inconsistencies. Are we repenting and turning toward Jesus, or are we ignoring Scripture and turning toward our own desires?

Discussion for Question 4: So Why Here?

1. What is the difference between joining the church and the local country club? For many people, joining either has very similar reasons: proximity to their home, their friends are members, their kids like it, it doesn't require much as long as you are current on your dues, and if you stick around long enough, you can be on the board of directors. Discuss.

2. Supporting the church in its "worship and work" is part of this vow. What is the worship of the church, and how do you support that? What is the work of the church, and how do you support that?

3. Invite your pastor or one of your church officers (elders or deacons in our tradition) and ask them what the "ideal" church member would look like to them?

4. Brainstorm as a class what you think a healthy amount of support toward the church would be (in terms of money and time). Also, on the other end, what might be a bit overboard in terms of expectations? Are there written or unwritten/understood expectations placed upon the members of your church?

5. Think for just a moment about your pastor's or church officers' spouses and children. Are there subtle expectations of a greater level of commitment from them toward the church? How many Sundays could one of them miss before you heard chatter and how many Sundays could you miss before you heard chatter?

6. Are you giving financially to the church? How do you determine the amount of your giving? Is your giving in *response to* and *in proportion to* what God has given you?

7. With a clear conscience, look at that phrase "to the best of your ability." This phrase should concurrently free you from guilt and also motivate you to further service. How does the same phrase do both? Are you serving in that way now?

Discussion for Question 5: I'm Saying What?!?

1. Submission is a difficult thing for all of us. Why do you think it was important to include a promise of submission to the government and discipline of the church right on the front end of church membership?
2. Do you find this offensive or encouraging?
3. Most of us "cross our fingers" when it comes to this vow. We put a mental asterisk at the end of the sentence and say that we "promise to submit to the government and discipline of the church ... until such time as we disagree with the government or the discipline of the church." Why does this vow primarily matter only when we disagree?
4. Why do we promise to submit to the church leadership? Why not simply promise to submit to God? Why have we historically said that they are one in the same?
5. Think of a difficult time or scenario where you had to submit to an authority in your life. What did God forge in your character as a result of that situation? Name several types of church scenarios where submission is difficult.
6. Why is church discipline necessary? Is church discipline only carried out in formal situations, or is it operative all the time? How is the preaching of the Word a type of discipline?
7. Steve Brown says, "We don't discipline church members for sin. If we did, then everyone would be under discipline *all the time!* We discipline for lack of repentance!" What does that mean? How do we formally and informally call the church to repentance on a public and private basis?
8. How do we protect the purity of the church? How do we concurrently protect the peace of the church? Can you ever have one without the other?
9. Talk about some ways that you can make sure you are "studying the purity and peace" of the church? What resources do you think might be helpful? How might you leverage this study toward future discussions?

Discussion for: Where the Rubber Hits the Road

1. Have each person privately write down their answer to this question and anonymously—because you want *real* answers—place their answers in a hat in the front of the room. The question is this: "What is one thing that could *never be changed* in this church without a big uproar? _____"

   Read the answers and have someone tally up the results.

2. Do the same thing again, but this time have class members answer this question: "If I could only change *one thing* about this church, it would be _____."

   Read the answers and have someone tally up the results.

3. Pass out one more sheet of paper and ask class members to list the item mentioned in either list that really rubbed them the wrong way. If something was called a "sacred cow" or if someone disliked hearing the *one thing* someone else wanted to change, why were they bothered? This should *not* be a discussion, just information at this point. *The next question will be a delicate discussion.*

4. Now ask the class to consider how so many different people with such varied and competing preferences are going to worship with and love one another for years to come. Don't allow your fellow classmates to dismiss the issues as small or insignificant. Remember each "issue" was someone's preference. If something gets brushed off, you should remember that someone sitting in that room said that was the *one thing* they wanted included or removed from their church.

5. Spend the remainder of the class talking about how loving one another means dying to our preferences in favor of something bigger than ourselves: the peace, purity, unity, and edification of the bride of Christ.

6. Have a group hug (kidding, kind of ...) and remind the class how much healthier it is to talk about these things in *this* context rather than having them bubble up during a church conflict.

Suggested Small Group Scope and Sequence

Small Group Discussion for Preface

1. What distinguishes church membership from membership in fraternal or social organizations?
2. What aspects of church membership are similar to membership in other organizations?
3. Get in groups and make a list of other organizations where people in those organizations must join the group to call themselves members.

   a. What are the membership criteria of those groups?
   b. What is required to keep active membership?
   f. Can someone lose his membership?
   g. Are there views or beliefs that would preclude someone from becoming a member of that group?
   h. Are there other organizations whose beliefs or views represent the polar opposite of these organizations?
   i. How does agreeing with or believing something provide the line of distinction between these two groups?

4. Make up a hypothetical group where membership could be granted. (This could be something like the "Chocolate Lovers Club.") In doing so what do you learn about the necessity of membership criteria or shared beliefs?
5. Why do you think some people react against standards or criteria when it comes to membership in a Christian church?
6. Who ultimately sets the standards for church membership? How are those standards implemented?
7. How could a low view or loose adherence to membership criteria actually contribute to the demise of an organization?
8. What is the difference between discriminating against certain people and determining membership criteria based on shared beliefs?

Group Exercise

Pass out a sheet of paper that has nothing printed on it except the original membership question for the specific week.

1.) Hands On: Have class members highlight or circle words or phrases in that question that they do not understand or do not particularly like.

2.) Discussion: Have class members share their circled phrases and thoughts/concerns about those phrases with the class.

3.) Teaching: Group leader should explain each phrase using the teaching from that particular chapter, other resources, and personal experience.

4.) Smaller Group Exercise: Break up into smaller groups (if practical) and have each smaller group choose one of the demographics below and rewrite the membership question into understandable language for those individuals: grade school, middle school, junior high/high school, college/career, young married, midlife, seniors. Feel free to delineate your own group parameters to your context more precisely. Have the smaller groups present their rewritten questions.

5.) Personal: Have class members individually rewrite the original question *as a statement* in their own words. This should be written as a personal declaration, not as a question. Allow class members to share their statements and observations about the entire exercise.

CPSIA information can be obtained at www.ICGtesting.com
Printed in the USA
LVOW07s2126111115

462177LV00001B/49/P

9 781490 838779